Relapse Prevention Workbook for Individuals with Psychosis

Understand Psychosis: Issues, Treatments, Challenges, and Self Management Tips.

Theo Gaius

This book is dedicated to everyone experiencing or recovery from psychosis.

Chapter One: Introduction

Around 50-70% of people with the first episode of psychosis relapse within two years of recovery. Relapse can have social and financial implications on the lives of individuals and their families. It can also have a significant adverse effect on self-esteem and may increase self-stigma. Therefore managing and minimizing relapse is an essential component in the treatment of people experiencing or recovery from psychosis.

The Relapse Prevention Workbook for Individuals with Psychosis is designed to help individuals develop a person-centered plan to help them recognize relapse signs and take full responsibility for their health and well-being. It involves learning more about oneself, understanding and reflecting on past experiences, developing skills to recognize signs of relapse, and finally putting together an action plan to prevent and manage relapse.

The idea behind self-management plans emanates from the principle that learning about oneself and developing a plan to prevent relapse will increase self-confidence, thereby giving the individual more personal control of their mental health well-being.

The overall treatment goal in psychosis management is to improve the individual functional capacity by focusing on social and vocational functioning. An effective relapse prevention plan will recognize and harness individual strengths and weaknesses to maintain social and occupational functioning.

The workbook is in two parts. The first part guides the user in preparing a person-centered relapse prevention plan. The second part discusses psychosis, treatment options, challenges, and self management tips, including how to support individuals experiencing or recovery from psychosis.

What is Psychosis

Psychosis is a medical term used to describe a condiion where an individual see or hear things that are not there or believes things that are not true. When an individual sees things that are not there or hears voices that are not there, it is called hallucination. When they believe something that cannot be true, it is called delusion. Examples of mental health problems included in this group are Schizophrenia and Schizo-affective disorder. The Schizo-affective disorder is when they have Schizophrenia and Bipolar disorder diagnosis and often referred to as dual diagnosis.

A majority of people will experience just one episode of psychosis, while over 50% of those people may experience further episodes of psychosis. When psychotic symptoms reappear and the person becomes unwell or become hospitalized, this event is called 'relapse.'

There are steps you can take to control and manage psychosis and take ownership of your recovery. You should understand that you are not alone, and other people may have similar problems or have had similar experiences as you. Therefore, it is crucial that you speak to people around you and not isolate yourself from friends, family, and available support services. People who have kept the problems secret have worsened their symptoms and on some occasions make very unwise decisions.It is essential that you speak to people and also seek available support.

This guide is an easy-to-read book aimed at individuals who have experienced some forms of psychosis and have relapsed or who fear they may relapse in the future. This guide will also be useful to mental health professionals who can use it to support their patients either in inpatient settings or in the community.

Early Warning Signs

The first step to managing any form of psychosis is recognizing signs that indicate a relapse is imminent, and those signs are collectively called "early warning signs".This step also includes understanding what relapse is and assessing your own knowledge of what it is. You might be experiencing relapse without even knowing it. It is important to note that relapse signs are specific to each individual, and they tend to follow a recognizable pattern each time the individual becomes unwell. Person A's early warning signs might be different from what person B experiences. Knowing the early warning signs and steps that lead up to a relapse can help you make healthy choices and take alternative action. These signs can occur slowly over time, sometimes weeks or months before relapse. They can present in the form of gradual change in behavior, thinking, or feelings.The individual may start to experience negative emotional responses, such as feeling anxious, concentrating issues, anger, and moodiness. They may also experience changes to sleep patterns, withdrawing from others, and feeling suspicious of people around them. It is important to recognize these signs as quickly as possible. This stage occurs before a person is even aware that they could be in danger of relapse, and intervening now can prevent the issue from taking hold.

It would help if you kept a diary of what triggers psychotic episodes in you. It could be lack of sleep, stress, low mood, family matters, financial issues, work stress. It could be anything.

You can also ask friends and family members or someone you trust to let you know if they notice changes in your mood or behavior. They can help you identify triggers they have observed in the past that make you become unwell and also things that appear to have helped you recover. Make a list of these triggers and take steps to avoid or manage them.

On a broad note, the following are some of the common early warning signs that I have heard from patients during my years working in mental health.

Common Early Warning Signs

Psychosis relapse early warning signs may vary between individuals, but there are some common signs to watch for. If you or someone you know is recovering from a psychotic episode, be vigilant for the following warning signs:

1. Sleep disturbances: Changes in sleep patterns, such as insomnia or oversleeping, can indicate an impending relapse.

2. Social withdrawal: Isolating oneself from friends, family, or other support systems can be an early sign of a relapse.

3. Mood changes: Sudden shifts in mood, including increased irritability, anxiety, or depression, can signal an upcoming relapse.

4. Increased sensitivity: Heightened sensitivity to sensory stimuli, such as bright lights, loud noises, or strong smells, can indicate an impending relapse.

5. Decline in functioning: A noticeable decline in the ability to perform daily tasks, work, or engage in social activities may be a sign of an impending relapse.

6. Deterioration of personal hygiene: Neglecting personal hygiene or grooming habits can be an early warning sign of relapse.

7. Suspiciousness or paranoia: An increase in suspicious or paranoid thoughts may signal a relapse.

8. Magical thinking: The return of unusual or irrational beliefs that are not grounded in reality can be an early warning sign.

9. Preoccupation with unusual ideas or thoughts: Becoming preoccupied with strange or unusual thoughts can be a sign of an impending relapse.

10. Auditory or visual hallucinations

11. Disorganized thoughts or speech: Difficulty organizing thoughts or speaking coherently can indicate a potential relapse.

12. Cognitive difficulties: Problems with memory, concentration, or decision-making can be early warning signs of a relapse.

13. Reduced insight: Failing to recognize one's own symptoms or the need for treatment may signal an impending relapse.

14. Increased substance use: Using drugs or alcohol to cope with symptoms can exacerbate psychosis and increase the risk of relapse.

15. Noncompliance with treatment: Skipping medications or therapy sessions can be a warning sign that a person is struggling to maintain their recovery.

16. Family or relationship stress: Conflict or stress in personal relationships can be a trigger for relapse.

17. Changes in appetite: Significant changes in appetite or weight can be an early warning sign of relapse.

18. Feelings of hopelessness or despair: Overwhelming feelings of hopelessness or thoughts of self-harm can signal a potential relapse.

If you or someone you know is experiencing these early warning signs of psychosis relapse, it is crucial to seek professional help immediately. Early intervention can help prevent a full-blown relapse and maintain progress in recovery.

Your own Early Warning Signs
Identifying personalized early warning signs of an impending relapse is crucial in maintaining progress and preventing a full-blown episode. These early warning signs can differ significantly between individuals, as they are influenced by personal experiences, cultural backgrounds, and other unique factors.

However, what matters is recognizing those signs that often lead to you becoming unwell and those changes in you before you relapse.

For example, Subtle changes in thoughts and feelings: Small shifts in the way you think or feel might be an indication of an impending relapse. These changes may be subtle and might not be immediately noticeable to others. It is essential to pay attention to any unusual thoughts or emotions and communicate them to a mental health professional.

Each person has unique routines and habits that help them maintain their mental well-being. Deviations from these routines, such as changes in sleeping patterns, eating habits, or exercise routines, can be early warning signs of relapse.

A decline in the quality or frequency of social interactions, or sudden changes in relationships with friends and family, can be an early warning sign of relapse. Maintaining supportive connections and being aware of changes in social dynamics can help prevent relapses.

The return of unusual thought patterns or beliefs that were present during a previous psychotic episode may signal an impending relapse. Identifying these thought patterns and addressing them with a mental health professional can help mitigate the risk of a relapse.

Each individual has specific coping mechanisms that help them manage their mental health. If you notice that your coping strategies are becoming less effective or that you're relying on unhealthy coping mechanisms, such as substance use, this could be an early warning sign of relapse.

To identify personalized early warning signs, consider the following strategies:

1. Self-monitoring: Pay close attention to your thoughts, feelings, and behaviors. Regularly assess how you're doing and whether you notice any changes that could signal an impending relapse. Keeping a journal can be an effective way to track your mental health and identify patterns over time.

2. Seek feedback from trusted individuals: Share your experiences and concerns with close friends, family members, or mental health professionals who are familiar with your history. They may be able to provide valuable insights and help you identify early warning signs that you might not notice on your own.

3. Create a relapse prevention plan: Develop a personalized plan to prevent relapses by identifying your unique early warning signs, triggers, and coping strategies. Work with your mental health care team to establish a clear plan of action for when these signs emerge. This can help you feel more in control and prepared for any potential relapse.

4. Attend therapy sessions: Regular therapy sessions can help you monitor your mental health and identify early warning signs. A mental health professional can provide guidance and support in addressing any concerns or changes you notice.

5. Stay informed: Educate yourself about psychosis and the recovery process. Understanding the condition and knowing what

to expect can help you identify potential warning signs and seek help when needed.

Once you've identified your personalized early warning signs, it's crucial to take action to prevent a relapse:

1. Maintain adherence to treatment: Follow your prescribed treatment plan, including taking medications as prescribed and attending therapy sessions. Consistency in treatment is vital for preventing relapses.
2. Develop healthy coping strategies: Engage in activities that promote mental well-being, such

Take, for example, creating a mood diary to track changes in your mood to help identify triggers.

After identifying your early warning signs, it is now time to create a clear plan about what you will do if you become aware of these signs. There is a range of things you can do to prevent the signs from escalating into relapse. Some of these things could be things you are already doing, but it is important to still add them to your plan.

For example, it could be basic things like:

When I feel stressed, I like to be on my own, or I like to take a bath.

When I start to feel like talking to myself, I like to walk in the park or visit friends or call family members.

Some of these items could be things that have worked in the past or just things you think will help you relax and not escalate into relapse.

It is also essential that you understand those stress triggers. For example, preparing for college exams can trigger stress which could lead to relapse. It may help to reflect on particular events that may have triggered psychosis to identify the exact trigger. The first step to managing triggers is to avoid them if you can. However, it is possible that avoiding these triggers could affect your quality of life, so it may not be possible to remove these triggers.

Having understood your early warning signs, the next step is to create a detailed crisis recovery plan,

Crisis Recovery Plan

A mental health crisis recovery plan, also known as a crisis plan or a safety plan, is a personalized document that outlines the steps to take and the resources to utilize when you or someone you care about is experiencing a mental health crisis. Creating a recovery plan can help you regain control, manage symptoms, and access appropriate support during difficult times. Here are the steps to create a mental health crisis recovery plan:

1. Recognize the warning signs: Identify the early warning signs that may indicate a mental health crisis is imminent. These may include changes in thoughts, feelings, or behaviors that signal a decline in mental well-being. Write these signs down as the first part of your plan.
2. List coping strategies: Write down healthy coping mechanisms that help you manage

14

stress, anxiety, or other symptoms. These strategies may include deep breathing exercises, mindfulness practices, physical activity, or engaging in a calming hobby. Make sure these coping strategies are easily accessible and realistic to implement during a crisis.

3. Establish a support network: Identify the people you can trust and reach out to during a crisis, such as friends, family members, mental health professionals, or support group members. Include their names, phone numbers, and any other relevant contact information in your plan.

4. Identify professional help: List the names and contact information of your mental health care providers, such as therapists, psychiatrists, and primary care physicians. Include crisis hotlines or emergency services that can provide immediate assistance during a mental health crisis, such as local crisis lines, national suicide hotlines, or the emergency room.

5. Specify medication information: Include details about any medications you are currently taking, such as the names, dosages, and prescribing doctor. This information can be crucial for healthcare providers to make informed decisions during a crisis.

6. Create a safe environment: Identify any potential hazards in your environment that could pose a risk during a mental health crisis, such as access to firearms, sharp objects, or harmful substances. Develop a plan to remove or secure these items during a crisis to ensure your safety and the safety of others around you.

7. Define self-care activities: Outline self-care practices that contribute to your overall well-being, such as maintaining a consistent sleep schedule, eating a balanced diet, engaging in regular physical activity, and staying connected with loved ones. Incorporating these practices into your daily routine can help build resilience and reduce the likelihood of a crisis.

8. Develop a post-crisis plan: Consider the steps you will take to recover and regain stability after a mental health crisis. This may involve scheduling follow-up appointments with mental health professionals, engaging in self-care practices, and re-establishing your daily routine. Having a plan in place can help you navigate the aftermath of a crisis more effectively.

9. Share your plan: Provide copies of your mental health crisis recovery plan to trusted friends, family members, or mental health care providers who may be involved in your care during a crisis. This ensures they are aware of your needs, preferences, and the steps to take if a crisis occurs.

10. Review and update your plan regularly: As your circumstances, mental health, and support network change over time, it's essential to review and update your crisis recovery plan accordingly. Regularly evaluate the plan's effectiveness and make adjustments as needed. Consider revisiting your plan every few months or after significant life events.

Creating a mental health crisis recovery plan is a proactive step in managing your mental health and ensuring that you have the necessary resources and support during difficult times. By recognizing warning signs, employing coping strategies, establishing a support network, and planning for both crisis and post-crisis situations, you can navigate mental health challenges more effectively and maintain control over your well-being. Remember, it's essential to keep open lines of communication with your mental health care providers, friends, and family so they can provide support and assistance when needed.

Chapter Two: How to Prevent Relapse

Network with others or Join a Peer Group

In a peer support group, you will engage with people who are currently experiencing or have experienced what you are dealing with now. Peer group is good because you hear other people's stories and gain an insight into how you can control and manage your psychosis. You can find local support groups in your area by contacting local services around you. Depending on your location, this could mean contacting mental health services, doctors, charities, and voluntary bodies.

Maintain relationships

Maintaining a good relationship with friends and family and the wider community also increases your self-confidence and makes you feel valued. This can help you cope in difficult times because having a connection with others helps promote self-worth and feelings of happiness

Feeling lonely and isolating oneself from people can often lead to emotional responses, such as anxiety, suicidal thoughts, stress, or even making your symptoms worse.

Look after your Physical Health
People who experience psychosis or other mental conditions tend to have poorer physical health than the general population. Many studies have been done on why individuals experiencing psychosis have poorer

physical health, and there are many factors for this. One factor was the individual lack of motivation to take responsibility for their physical health.

Have Enough Sleep

There is a link between sleep and mental health, and sleep disturbance often worsens mental health. Sleep disturbance comes in various forms. You may be finding it hard to fall asleep, staying asleep every time, or waking up earlier than you'd like to

Getting enough sleep is very important because it gives you the energy to cope with difficult feelings and experiences throughout the day. Lack of sleep can make you feel a lot worse and heighten anxiety. If you don't sleep, you could find it difficult to concentrate on making plans and decisions. It can also make you feel irritable, making it difficult to cope with day-to-day life, such as work or with family and friends.

Certain factors can affect your sleep, like stress at work or the type of work you do. For example, working a night shift work pattern means you have to stay awake at night and try to catch up with sleep during the day, making it difficult for you to cope. Family problems, money matters and worries, poor housing, and medication can also affect sleep patterns.

Psychiatric medication can sometimes induce insomnia and or other sleep disturbances, including nightmares and oversleeping. It is important to note that stopping psychiatric drugs can also cause sleep problems.

All these could trigger sleep disturbances. If you think these may be affecting your sleep, I would suggest you see a doctor to discuss alternative options. Your doctor could ask you to attend sleep groups, see a psychologist or prescribe you medications to help you sleep. There are other self-help therapies for sleep that you can discuss with your doctor, local mental health team, or pharmacist.

Eat Healthily and Drink Adequate Fluid

Also, think about your diet, eat healthily and avoid food that can increase or decrease your blood sugar levels drastically, such as sweets, biscuits, and sugary or alcoholic drinks. Eat regularly and drink an adequate amount of water. Not eating regularly or enough food can affect your blood sugar levels. Research studies have shown that a decreased blood sugar level can affect your mood, making you feel tired, irritable, which can lead to depression and other forms of physical health conditions.

Engage in Physical Activities

Participate in physical activities and exercise regularly as you can. You can even join a local walking group in your area.Cycle if you can, engage in running activities, or use recreational activities such as swimming pools if you enjoy swimming. Involve yourself in various physical activities because they are helpful for your mental wellbeing.

It is also important to avoid illicit drugs and substances.These are sometimes used to cope with anxiety and depression but in the long term can have devastating effects. Alcohol can be used in much the same way.

Chapter Three: Supporting Someone Experiencing Psychotic Symptoms

How Long Does Psychosis Last?

Psychosis can result in hallucinations, where a person sees, hears, tastes, or feels things that aren't actually there. It can also present as delusions, where a person strongly believes something to be true despite it going against what is generally accepted or reality. It can also present as disorganized or confused thinking, speech or behaviors.

The psychosis duration and recovery time will depend on how the person experiences psychosis and what induces the psychotic episode. Psychosis can be brought on by mental health issues such as bipolar disorder or schizophrenia, but it can also be the result of drug use.

Psychosis Stages

There are three stages of psychosis: prodrome, acute and recovery.

Prodrome phase: During the prodromal stage of psychosis, the person will start having changes in behavior or perceptions that might indicate psychosis is about to occur. During the beginning stages of psychosis, the person may have a hard time focusing on what they are doing or thinking, feel easily overwhelmed, have disturbances in their sleep, want to be alone more than usual or seclude themselves from social events.

Acute phase: Acute psychosis refers to the stage where hallucinations, delusions, or other unusual behaviors are occurring. These symptoms are usually debilitating and can interfere with a person's normal life. How long acute psychosis lasts depends on whether the psychosis is related to a mental health disorder or substance-induced.

Recovery: The last stage of psychosis is recovery. During this stage, the symptoms of psychosis will lessen and the person will be able to return to a normal routine. This phase usually occurs after the person receives treatment for their mental health disorder or stops using the substance that induced psychosis.

Length of Different Types of Psychosis
The duration of psychosis depends on the type and cause of the psychotic episode. For instance, the duration of psychosis associated with a mental health disorder is different from that of drug-induced psychosis. Additionally, with mental health disorders, the length of time psychosis lasts will vary.

A brief psychotic disorder lasts for one month or less and usually only occurs once, whereas schizophrenia is defined by symptoms or its precursors that lasts for a period of six months. Additionally, two or more symptoms, such as hallucinations, delusions, disorganized speech and extremely disorganized or catatonic behavior, must be significant and last for at least one month. In bipolar disorder, a person may experience psychosis during the manic phase, which can have a duration of weeks to months.

Can Psychosis Go Away on Its Own?

If the psychosis is a one-time event, such as with brief psychotic episode, or substance-induced psychosis, it may disappear on its own. However, if the psychosis is a result of an underlying mental health disorder, it is unlikely the psychosis will cease naturally. Studies have found that shortening the time between the first psychotic episode and when a person receives treatment can help improve their overall success with treatment. The length of time for psychosis to go away following the start of treatment can also be shortened by seeking treatment early after symptoms start to occur.

When to Seek Help

When a person experiences psychosis for the first time, it may be difficult to know if they should seek help or not. However, it has been shown that psychosis treatment greatly improves the sooner someone gets help. Therefore, if a person experiences psychosis that is not related to substance use, it would be beneficial for them to establish care with a trusted provider so that they can monitor their symptoms and receive treatment

For individuals that experience psychosis with substance use, it is generally a sign of a substance use disorder as this will usually only occur with chronic substance use. In many cases, getting treatment for their substance use disorder and stopping the use of the substance will improve their symptoms of psychosis.

People developing a psychotic disorder will often not reach out for help. Someone who is experiencing profound and frightening psychotic symptoms will often try to keep them a secret. If you are concerned about someone, approach the person in a caring and non-judgmental manner to discuss your concerns. The person you are trying to help might not trust you or might be afraid of being perceived as "different", and therefore may not be open with you. If possible, you should approach the person privately about their experiences in a place that is free of distractions.

Try to tailor your approach and interaction to the way the person is behaving (e.g. if the person is suspicious and is avoiding eye contact, be sensitive to this and give them the space they need). Do not touch the person without their permission. You should state the specific behaviours you are concerned about and should not speculate about the person's diagnosis. It is important to allow the person to talk about their experiences and beliefs if they want to. As far as possible, let the person set the pace and style of the interaction. You should recognize they may be frightened by their thoughts and feelings. Ask the person about what will help them to feel safe and in control. Reassure them you are there to help and support them, and you want to keep them safe. If possible, offer the person choices of how you can help them so they are in control. Convey a message of hope by assuring them help is available and things can get better.

If the person is unwilling to speak with you, do not try to force them to talk about their experiences. Rather, let them know you will be available if they would like to talk in the future.

How can I be supportive?

Treat the person with respect. You should try to empathize with how the person feels about their

29

beliefs and experiences without stating any judgments about the content of those beliefs and experiences. The person may be behaving and talking differently due to psychotic symptoms. They may also find it difficult to distinguish between what is real from what is not real.

You should avoid confronting the person and should not criticize or blame them. Understand the symptoms for what they are and try not to take them personally. Do not use sarcasm and try to avoid using patronizing statements. It is important for you to be honest when interacting with the person. Do not make any promises you cannot keep.

How do I deal with delusions (false beliefs) and hallucinations (perceiving things that are not real)?

It is important to recognize that the delusions and hallucinations are very real to the person. You should not dismiss, minimize or argue with the person about their delusions or hallucinations. Similarly, do not act alarmed, horrified or embarrassed by the person's delusions or hallucinations.

You should not laugh at the person's symptoms of psychosis. If the person exhibits paranoid behaviour, do not encourage or inflame the person's paranoia.

How do I deal with communication difficulties?

People experiencing symptoms of psychosis are often unable to think clearly.You should respond to disorganized speech by communicating in an uncomplicated and succinct manner, and should repeat things if necessary. After you say something, you should be patient and allow plenty of time for the person to process the information and respond. If the person is showing a limited range of feelings, you should be aware it does not mean that the person is not feeling anything. Likewise, you should not assume the person cannot understand what you are saying, even if their response is limited.

Should I encourage the person to seek professional help?

You should ask the person if they have felt this way before and if so, what they have done in the past that has been helpful. Try to find out what type of assistance they believe will help them. Also, try to determine whether the person has a supportive social network and if they do, encourage them to utilize these supports.

If the person decides to seek professional help, you should make sure they are supported both emotionally and practically in accessing services. If the person does seek help, and either they or you lack confidence in the medical advice they have received, they should seek a second opinion from another medical or mental health professional.

What if the person doesn't want help?
The person may refuse to seek help even if they realize they are unwell. Their confusion and fear about what is happening to them may lead them to deny anything is wrong. In this case you should encourage them to talk to someone they trust. It is also possible a person may refuse to seek help because they lack insight that they are unwell. They might actively resist your attempts to encourage them to seek help. In either case, your course of action should depend on the type and severity of the person's symptoms.

It is important to recognize that unless a person with psychosis meets the criteria for involuntary committal procedures, they cannot be forced into treatment. If they are not at risk of harming themselves or others, you should remain patient, as people experiencing psychosis often need time to develop insight regarding their illness. Never threaten the person with the mental health act or hospitalization. Instead remain friendly and open to the possibility that they may want your help in the future.

What should I do in a crisis situation?
It is important the first aider take appropriate action and arrange for professional help if someone is at risk of harming themselves or someone else, even if the

person does not want help at that time. This may be a mental health professional, but include emergency medical services, the police or other professionals.

In a crisis situation, you should try to remain as calm as possible. Evaluate the situation by assessing the risks involved (e.g. whether there is any risk the person will harm themselves or others). It is important to assess whether the person is at risk of suicide. If the person has an advance directive or relapse prevention plan, you should follow those instructions. Try to find out if the person has anyone s/he trusts (e.g. close friends, family) and try to enlist their help. You should also assess whether it is safe for the person to be alone and, if not, should ensure someone stays with him or her.

It is important to communicate to the person in a clear and concise manner and use short, simple sentences. Speak quietly in a non-threatening tone of voice at a moderate pace. If the person asks you questions, answer them calmly. You should comply with requests unless they are unsafe or unreasonable. This gives the person the opportunity to feel somewhat in control.

You should be aware the person might act upon a delusion or hallucination. Remember your primary task is to de-escalate the situation and therefore you should not do anything to further agitate the person. Try to maintain safety and protect the person, yourself and others around you from harm. Make sure you have access to an exit.

You must remain aware you may not be able to de-escalate the situation and if this is the case, you should be prepared to call for assistance. If the person is at risk of harming themselves or others, you should call for assistance (e.g. emergency services 911) to ensure they are evaluated by a medical or mental health professional as soon as possible. You should convey specific, concise observations about the severity of the person's behaviour and symptoms to the emergency services dispatcher and to emergency services personnel when they arrive at the scene. (Note: you should not assume the person is experiencing a psychotic episode but should rather outline any symptoms and immediate concerns.) You should tell the emergency services whether or not the person is armed. You should explain to the person you are helping who any unfamiliar people are, that they are there to help and how they are going to help.

What if the person becomes aggressive?

People experiencing a psychosis are not usually aggressive and are at a much higher risk of harming themselves than others. However, certain symptoms of psychosis (e.g. delusions or hallucinations) can cause people to become aggressive. You should know how to de-escalate the situation if the person you are trying to help becomes aggressive.

How to de-escalate the situation:

- Do not respond in a hostile, disciplinary or challenging manner to the person.
- Do not threaten them as this may increase fear or prompt aggressive behaviour.
- Avoid raising your voice or talking too fast.
- Stay calm and avoid nervous behaviour (e.g. shuffling your feet, fidgeting, making abrupt movements).
- Do not restrict the person's movement (e.g. if he or she wants to pace up and down the room).
- Remain aware the person's symptoms or fear causing their aggression might be exacerbated if you take certain steps (e.g. involve the police).
- Take any threats or warnings seriously, particularly if the person believes they are being persecuted. If you are frightened, seek outside help immediately. You should never put yourself at risk. Similarly, if the person's aggression escalates out of control at any time, you should remove yourself from the situation and call emergency services.

Finally , Take care of yourself: Supporting someone with psychosis can be emotionally challenging and draining. Ensure you also take care of your own mental and physical well-being. Seek support from friends, family, or mental health professionals, and engage in self-care practices to maintain your resilience and ability to provide effective support.

Be patient with the recovery process: Recovery from psychosis can be a slow and nonlinear process. Be patient and understanding as your loved one navigates their journey, and recognize that setbacks can occur. Continue offering your support and encouragement throughout their recovery.

By following these tips, you can provide valuable support to someone experiencing psychotic symptoms. Remember, empathy, understanding, and patience are key to helping your loved one navigate this challenging time and work towards recovery.

Page left Blank

You can add a note here

Chapter Four: Technology to Prevent Relapse

Technology can be a valuable tool in supporting someone experiencing psychotic symptoms. There are various ways technology can be utilized to provide assistance, monitor symptoms, and enhance the overall recovery process:

Telehealth and teletherapy: Telehealth allows individuals to access mental health care services remotely through videoconferencing or phone calls. This can be particularly beneficial for those who have limited access to in-person care or feel more comfortable discussing their experiences in a familiar environment.

Mental health apps: Many mental health apps are available that can help individuals track their symptoms, monitor their mood, practice relaxation techniques, and access helpful resources. These apps can also serve as useful tools for self-management and self-care.

Online support groups: Online forums, social media groups, or chat rooms can provide individuals with a safe space to connect with others who have similar experiences, share their stories, and find support. These virtual communities can help reduce feelings of isolation and provide a sense of belonging.

Virtual reality therapy: Virtual reality (VR) technology can be used in therapeutic settings to help individuals confront and manage their symptoms in a controlled environment. For example, VR can be utilized for exposure therapy to help individuals face their fears or anxieties.

Wearable devices: Wearable technology, such as fitness trackers or smartwatches, can help monitor physical health indicators, sleep patterns, and activity levels, providing valuable insights into an individual's overall well-being. These devices can help identify potential triggers or stressors and support the development of healthier habits.

Electronic medication reminders: Adherence to medication is crucial in managing psychotic symptoms. Smartphone apps or digital pill dispensers can be used to set up reminders, ensuring that individuals take their medications on time and in the correct dosage.

Online resources and educational materials: The internet offers a wealth of resources, including articles, videos, and webinars, that can help individuals and their support network better understand psychosis and its treatment options. Access to reliable and up-to-date information can empower individuals to make informed decisions about their care.

Crisis intervention and support services: Technology can facilitate access to crisis support services, such as online chat support, text-based helplines, or national crisis hotlines. These resources can provide immediate assistance during a mental health crisis and connect individuals with the appropriate help.

Remote monitoring and digital interventions: Some mental health care providers use remote monitoring technology to track an individual's symptoms, medication adherence, and overall progress. This data can help inform treatment decisions and allow for timely intervention if symptoms worsen.

Digital therapeutics: Digital therapeutics are evidence-based interventions delivered through digital platforms, such as mobile apps, web-based programs, or virtual reality systems. They can provide personalized, data-driven treatment options that complement traditional therapy and medication.

By leveraging technology, individuals experiencing psychotic symptoms and their support networks can access a range of tools and resources that help manage symptoms, facilitate recovery, and improve overall well-being. It is essential to ensure that any technology used is evidence-based, reliable, and respects the individual's privacy and security. Additionally, it's important to remember that technology should not replace professional mental health care but rather serve as a supplementary tool to enhance traditional treatment approaches. Always consult with a mental health care provider before incorporating new technology into an individual's treatment plan to ensure its appropriateness and effectiveness.

Chapter Five: The Difference Between A Panic Attack Vs Psychosis

For people who do not know what a panic attack is, when they see a victim having an attack, they tend to immediately think that the victim is having a heart attack or a mental problem. Although the difference may not seem very apparent, the differences exist nonetheless. If you suffer from panic attacks, then it is crucial for you to understand the difference between the two if you ever want to recover from the stigma attached to this disorder.

Knowing the Difference

The key difference between panic attacks and psychosis is that a panic attack is a result of how the person reacts to sudden extreme stress or fear; whereas psychosis is hard wired into a person's brain. Although panic attacks happen very suddenly, they tend to have a trigger or a signal attached to it. Most sufferers would be able to tell you why they are having an attack; while those suffering from psychosis would not even know they are having a psychotic episode. Psychosis takes over the victim's mind almost completely so as to prevent them from telling right from wrong.

As most psychosis victims do not know that is happening and cannot control themselves during a psychotic episode, they need to be under constant observation by medical professionals, as they may pose a danger to people around them and also to themselves. A panic attack victim in general never poses danger to people around them as during an attack they are usually helpless.

Treatment for Panic Attacks and Psychosis
There is a huge difference between how a panic disorder is treated versus psychosis. In most cases, panic disorder can be treated with some mild anti-depression medication and if needed some therapy sessions. On the other hand, psychosis requires far more attention and this includes stronger anti-

psychotic medication, frequent psychiatric consultations and for very severe cases, hospitalisation.

When deciding a treatment for either disorder, medical health professionals must first determine the severity of both and whether or not the victim poses harm to people around them and to themselves. No matter how severe the condition for the disorder is, there are always treatment options available.

Drug-induced Psychosis

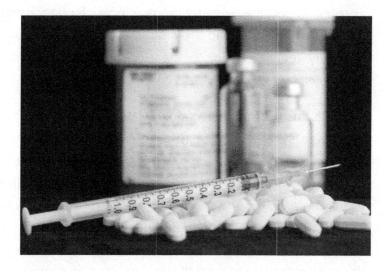

Psychosis is a mental health problem which temporarily causes someone to interpret the world differently from those around them. Drug-induced psychosis, also known as 'stimulant psychosis', refers to any psychotic episode which has been caused by abuse of stimulants, an adverse reaction to prescription drugs, or excessive use of alcohol which has directly triggered a psychotic reaction.

Psychosis is often characterised by delusions or hallucinations, which are experiences that are far removed from reality. Delusions are irrational beliefs that a person holds, even when they are presented with evidence that contradicts these beliefs. Delusions may include believing that you have a serious or life-threatening physical illness, that you are responsible for terrible things happening to other people, or that you are bankrupt when you are not. Hallucinations refer to intense sensory perceptions of phenomena that are not real, and are characterised by individuals vividly feeling, seeing or hearing things that do not truly exist.

Drugs such as cocaine, cannabis and hallucinogens can worsen symptoms of existing mental illnesses, whilst taking such substances for a long period of time can also see you develop symptoms of psychosis, including paranoia. If you are diagnosed with drug-induced psychosis and have a dependency on alcohol or drugs, you may have what is called a dual diagnosis, whereby your underlying mental illness will need to be treated independently of any substance addiction.

What Causes Someone to Develop Drug-induced Psychosis?

Drug-induced psychosis can happen when you take too much of a certain drug, so that its level of toxicity provokes paranoia and a psychotic episode. It can also occur when if you have an adverse reaction from mixing different substances, or withdrawing from a drug, prescribed or otherwise. You may already have underlying mental health conditions such as bipolar disorder or schizophrenia, where delusions and hallucinations are associated symptoms, with psychotic episodes resulting from substance use, indicating that you may be prone to psychosis.

If your psychosis has been triggered through drug use in order to cope with underlying mental illness, a diagnosis would need to determine whether symptoms would continue without the drug present, as this would not be drug-related psychosis. Drug-induced psychosis is more apparent when your symptoms wear off after you have stopped using the drug, while the initial symptoms such as social withdrawal and lack of motivation may gradually build to include delusions or hallucinations.

Treatment for Drug-induced Psychosis

If you are diagnosed with drug-induced psychosis, it is vitally important that you seek treatment from specialist medical professionals. Experienced therapists and consultants are trained in treating drug-induced psychosis, and can offer you a safe and understanding treatment environment as part of a bespoke treatment plan, which is aimed at reducing associated symptoms of psychosis and drug addiction, before targeting any underlying health issues which may have been triggered by substance abuse.

Treatment for Co-occurring Conditions

While removal of the drug from your system may remove symptoms of psychosis, if you have an underlying mental health condition such as anxiety or depression which prompted excessive use of a drug, or you have also been diagnosed with an existing psychotic disorder such as bipolar disorder or schizophrenia, further treatment will be required to address these conditions.

Therapies and medication can be offered on an inpatient, outpatient or day care basis depending on your circumstances, and may include:

Cognitive behavioural therapy (CBT) - once you have been medically stabilised, the practical and problem-solving talking therapy, CBT, can help you to learn more about the thoughts and moods that you experience before psychotic episodes occur, helping you to manage your emotions and paranoia more readily, and be aware of triggers.

If a mental health condition such as anxiety or depression exists, which has been masked by extensive use of drugs or alcohol to the point of psychosis, then CBT can help you to learn techniques to cope with and reduce associated symptoms so as to prevent relapse.

Family therapy - due to the serious nature of drug-induced psychosis and associated psychotic conditions, family therapy involving those closest to you, can help to ensure that there is sufficient support available at home to prevent relapse and manage associated symptoms, potentially reducing the need for extensive hospital treatment.

Anti-psychotic medication – if your underlying mental health condition features psychotic episodes as a symptom, then antidepressant, anti-psychotic or other medications such as clozapine (Clozaril) may be recommended for an extended period of time, particularly if delusions and hallucinations are frequent or particularly severe.

Chapter Six: Psychotic Depression

Whether you are in a place where you are dealing with depression or you know someone who is, you may find that there are other issues that can make things even more difficult. More to the point, if you find that psychotic depression is something that you are dealing with, either in yourself or in others, there are some facts that you need to know! Take a moment to thoroughly understand what psychotic depression is all about and to figure out what you need to know about it.

In the first place, psychotic depression is a subset of major depression, where the depression has a co-existing form of psychosis. In this case, psychosis is defined as a flawed view of reality. You may find that some of the symptoms of psychosis include delusions, visual hallucinations or auditory hallucinations. This can be a situation that is extremely convincing and frightening and about one in four people who are hospitalized for depression might fall under the umbrella term of psychotic depression.

When looking to diagnose psychotic depression, you will find that the full range of clinical depression symptoms are there as well. Things like feeling hopeless or worthless, fatigue and self loathing are certainly there, but you will also find that irrational thoughts and fears and the propensity for seeing and hearing things that are not real is present as well. In many cases, especially when things are very rough and when there has been a major upset in the life of the sufferer, it is not out of the question for hospitalization to be necessary.

If you are dealing with someone who is experiencing psychotic depression, you will find that the first and most important thing that you need to do is to get them to a situation where they cannot harm the people around them or themselves. People who are psychotic may not be able to tell fantasy from reality or they may become obsessed with a certain concept and refuse to let it go. They may feel as though the people around them are trying to harm them or that they need to protect themselves and their family from dangers that only they know about. Take a moment to consider what they might be going through.

CBT for Psychosis

Cognitive behaviour therapy (CBT) is a form of talking therapy. It focuses on thoughts and feelings and behaviours and how these affect each other. It is based on the idea that ways of thinking and behaviour can help cause mental health problems, or help to keep them going. CBT therapists aim to help people to improve their mental health through making changes in their thinking and behaviour. In psychosis, the aim is to reduce the distress caused by hallucinatory voices, and improve coping.

CBT involves a collaborative approach between patient and therapist. Both patient and therapist have an active part role.

At the beginning of CBT the patient and the therapist agree what problems to work on, and some specific goals.

Patient and therapist then work together to develop a 'case formulation'. This is a set of hypotheses which attempts to explain how the patient's problems have come about and what keeps them going. The formulation is then used to identify changes in thinking or behaviour that may be helpful.

A wide variety of techniques are used to change thinking and behaviour. Often these begin with self-monitoring, for example keeping a diary of thoughts and feelings. Different forms of CBT differ in how much emphasis is put on thoughts and how much on behaviour. Techniques may involve identifying and challenging negative thoughts, unhelpful beliefs and assumptions or experimenting with different behaviours and monitoring their effects. Some of the work of CBT is done between sessions, as 'homework'.

CBT sessions are structured. They usually begin with agreeing an agenda of what is to be discussed in the session and a review of any homework. They generally end with a review of the session and maybe agreeing homework for the following week.

In CBT for psychosis, the emphasis early on is on trying to create a good therapeutic relationship, so that the patient feels able and willing to engage in the work to be done. Therapists provide information about psychosis, and in particular try to make clear how psychotic experiences lie on a continuum with non-psychotic experience. This is called 'normalizing'. The latter stages of therapy will usually focus on relapse prevention. It is considered very important that the patient is offered hope and belief in the possibility of recovery.

CBT therapists have traditionally been active researchers, and there has been much more research into CBT than other forms of therapy. The research suggests that compared with standard care, CBT may reduce readmissions to hospital, reduce symptom severity, improve depression, social functioning and negative symptoms.

Antipsychotic Drugs

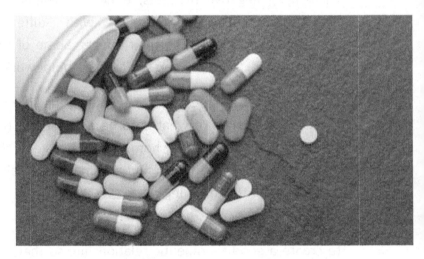

Antipsychotic drug are any agent used in the treatment of mental illness. Psychosis can affect cognitive processes such as judgment and frequently cause delusions and hallucinations. Effective treatments for some forms of schizophrenia have revolutionized thinking about the disease and have prompted investigations into its possible genetic origins and pathological causes. These investigations have also shed light on the mechanisms by which antipsychotic drugs exert their effects.

Another class of antipsychotic drugs, the phenothiazines, arose from modifications of the dye methylene blue, which was under investigation as an antagonist of histamine. Attempts to modify this series to increase their activity in the central nervous system and reduce the need for surgical anesthetics ultimately led to the first effective drug of this class, chlorpromazine. Its ability to stabilize behaviour and to improve lucidity as well as to reduce hallucinatory behaviour was recognized within a few years of its introduction in the mid-1950s. The use of chlorpromazine changed the role of the mental hospital and resulted in the large-scale, perhaps excessive, discharge of persons with schizophrenia into the outside world.

A third class of antipsychotics, the butyrophenones, emerged when a small Belgian drug company embarked on a plan in the late 1950s to develop analogs of meperidine through inexpensive chemical substitutions. Experiments gave rise to a compound that caused chlorpromazine-like sedation but had a completely different structure. This led to the compound haloperidol, a more powerful antipsychotic with relatively fewer side effects.

A fourth class of drugs, commonly known as "atypicals" but more properly called atypical antipsychotics or serotonin-dopamine antagonists, is related to chlorpromazine and to haloperidol. These antipsychotics can improve both the so-called positive symptoms (e.g., hallucinations, delusions, and agitation) and the negative symptoms of schizophrenia, such as catatonia and flattening of the ability to experience emotion. Each agent in this group has a unique profile of receptor interactions. Virtually all antipsychotics block dopamine receptors and reduce dopaminergic transmission in the forebrain. The atypical antipsychotics also have affinity for serotonin receptors.

The major acute side effects of chlorpromazine and haloperidol are oversedation and a malaise that makes the drugs poorly received by the patient and makes compliance with chronic self-medication difficult. Prolonged treatment of middle-aged and even young adults with antipsychotic drugs can evoke serious movement disorders that in part resemble Parkinson disease, a degenerative condition of the nerves. First to appear are tremors and rigidity, and those are followed by more complex movement disorders commonly associated with involuntary twitching movements on the arms, lips, and tongue, called tardive dyskinesia. The atypical antipsychotics do not produce the movement disorders that are seen with the use of the older drugs, probably because of their affinity for both serotonin and dopamine receptors. None of the antipsychotics is curative, because none eliminates the fundamental disorder of thought processes.

Neuroleptic malignant syndrome is a rare, potentially fatal neurological side effect of antipsychotic drug use. Individuals develop a severe rigidity with catatonia, autonomic instability, and stupor, which may persist for more than one week. Neuroleptic malignant syndrome has occurred with all antipsychotics, but the disorder is more common with relatively high doses of more potent agents such as haloperidol.

Mental Health - What's That?
Mental Health is about finding a balance between dealing with the difficulties in life and using the opportunities life presents for further development. Mental power is primary in helping create good things in our life, and is the vehicle that helps us work toward our hopes, dreams and aspirations. Mental health is far more than the absence of mental illness and has to do with many aspects of our lives including our physical health and well being.

Anxiety, stress and depression can make coping difficult for seniors who are often facing the physical, emotional and economic changes associated with aging. For instance, everyone with hypertension, diabetes, or asthma cope maladaptive to stress and they may have anxiety issues. Most people with an anxiety disorder will try to avoid exposure to whatever triggers their anxiety.

In anxiety disorders, people tend to get anxious when they are faced with a particular situation. So, for example, as a mental health nurse you could be helping to care and support a mother with severe post-natal depression, young man facing the complexities of a mental illness such as schizophrenia, someone experiencing anxiety and panic attacks which prevent them from functioning normally.

Depression, the fastest-growing cause of long-term disability in Canada, is the most common among this type of disorder, which includes bipolar disorder (also known as manic depression), dysthymia, and seasonal affective disorder. The research team has also found that stress at work is associated with a 50 per cent excess risk of coronary heart disease, and there is consistent evidence that jobs with high demands, low control, and effort-reward imbalance are risk factors for mental and physical health problems (major depression, anxiety disorders, and substance use disorders).

With mental health problems affecting one in four people in this region, and now among the main reasons for absence from work, no-one can afford to be blasé about their own mental health - or that of their friends, family or colleagues. The Mental Power Foundation uses research and practical projects to help people survive, recover from and prevent mental health problems. Mental health problems are painful -

emotionally, physically, spiritually and socially. Stress, depression and panic attacks are common conditions and they can all be successfully treated.

Chapter Seven: Myths About Psychosis

There are several myths and misconceptions about psychosis that can contribute to stigma and misunderstanding. Some common myths include:

Myth: People with psychosis are dangerous and violent.

Fact: The majority of people experiencing psychosis are not violent. While some individuals may exhibit aggressive behaviors during a psychotic episode, they are more likely to be frightened, confused, or withdrawn. It is important to remember that people with psychosis are more likely to be victims of violence than perpetrators.

Myth: Psychosis is the same as schizophrenia.

Fact: Psychosis is a symptom that can occur in various mental health conditions, including schizophrenia, bipolar disorder, and major depressive disorder. Schizophrenia is a specific mental health diagnosis that involves a range of symptoms, including persistent psychosis, disorganized thinking, and negative symptoms like reduced emotional expression or motivation.

Myth: People with psychosis have split personalities or multiple personalities.

Fact: Psychosis and dissociative identity disorder (formerly known as multiple personality disorder) are distinct mental health conditions. Psychosis involves a loss of contact with reality, while dissociative identity disorder is characterized by the presence of two or more distinct personality states that take control of a person's behavior.

Myth: Psychosis is a result of a weak character or personal failing.

Fact: Psychosis is a complex mental health condition with various contributing factors, including genetic, biological, and environmental factors. It is not a result of a weak character or personal failing, and blaming the individual for their symptoms only perpetuates stigma and misunderstanding.

Myth: People with psychosis cannot recover or lead fulfilling lives.

Fact: With appropriate treatment and support, many people who experience psychosis can recover and lead meaningful, productive lives. Treatment may include medication, therapy, and psychosocial interventions, all of which can help manage symptoms and promote recovery. It is essential to recognize that the recovery journey is unique for each individual and may involve setbacks and challenges. However, with persistence, support, and appropriate care, people with psychosis can achieve a significant degree of symptom management and improved quality of life.

Myth: Psychosis only affects adults.

Fact: Psychosis can affect people of all ages, including children and adolescents. Early-onset psychosis, which occurs before the age of 18, is less common but can have a significant impact on a young person's development and well-being. Early intervention and treatment are crucial for minimizing the long-term effects of psychosis in young people.

Myth: People with psychosis should be isolated from society.

Fact: Social support and meaningful connections are essential components of recovery for individuals with psychosis. Isolating people with psychosis can exacerbate symptoms and hinder recovery. Encouraging social engagement, fostering supportive relationships, and promoting community integration can all contribute to better outcomes for people experiencing psychosis.

By debunking these myths and promoting a better understanding of psychosis, we can help reduce stigma, encourage open conversations about mental health, and support individuals affected by psychosis in their recovery journey. Remember, education and empathy are key

Behavioral Health vs. Mental Health

Mental health, as defined by the World Health Organization, is "a state of well-being in which every individual realizes his or her own potential, can cope with the normal stresses of life, can work productively and fruitfully, and is able to make a contribution to his or her community." Your mental health encompasses a number of factors, such as your biology, your psychological condition, and your habits. Your behavioral health, on the other hand, examines how your habits impact your overall physical and mental wellbeing.

Behavioral and Mental Health Disorders

It can help to think of behavioral health as a subset of mental health, in that not all mental health disorders are a result of behavioral issues. Some of them are caused by brain chemistry or genetic inheritance. A short list of mental disorders that are not directly related to or caused by behaviors are:

Bipolar disorder

Schizophrenia

Depression

Generalized anxiety disorder

By contrast, behavioral health disorders result from maladaptive behaviors that negatively impact your physical or mental condition. Some examples of behavioral health disorders are:

Substance abuse

Gambling

Sex addiction

Eating disorders

CONCLUSION

Conversely, while many mental health conditions have a biological basis, they can still be severely impacted by your behaviors, in both positive and negative ways. Maladaptive behaviors – such as drinking, using drugs, or overeating – can exacerbate symptoms of a mental health disorder. On the flipside, developing effective coping mechanisms – such as exercising or meditating – can improve both your physical and mental state.

Obtaining the Right Diagnosis and Treatment .

Whether you're concerned about your mental health, your behavioral health, or both, it's crucial to obtain the correct diagnosis for your condition. All too often, it can be easy for inexperienced care providers to focus on behavior modification while overlooking underlying psychiatric conditions, or to treat a mental illness with medication while ignoring the need to change bad habits. The most effective treatment plan is one that takes a collaborative approach, employing a team of experts to consider all aspects of a patient's wellbeing. Treatment is often multi-faceted and can include medical interventions, cognitive behavioral therapy, group counseling, and more.

Collaborative care is especially important when it comes to a dual diagnosis – that is, a behavioral health disorder, such as substance abuse, that co-occurs with a mental health condition. Working together, a well-rounded team of doctors, nurses and therapists can ensure a patient is getting the best possible treatment to help them live their best life.

References

1. Wykes T, Steel C, Everitt B, Tarrier N. Cognitive behavior therapy for schizophrenia: effect sizes, clinical models, and methodological rigor. Schizophr Bull. 2008;34:523-537.

2. Freeman D. Improving cognitive treatments for delusions. Schizophr Res. 2011;132:135-139.

3. Clark DM. Developing new treatments: on the interplay between theories, experimental science and clinical innovation. Behav Res Ther. 2004;42:1089-1104.

4. Freeman D, Garety PA, Kuipers E, et al. A cognitive model of persecutory delusions. Br J Clin Psychol. 2002;41(pt 4):331-347.

5. Morrison AP. The interpretation of intrusions in psychosis: an integrative cognitive approach to hallucinations and delusions. Behav Cogn Psychother. 2001;29:257-276.

6. Chadwick P, Birchwood M. The omnipotence of voices. A cognitive approach to auditory hallucinations. Br J Psychiatry. 1994;164:190-201.

7. Beck AT, Rector NA, Stolar NM, Grant PM. Schizophrenia: Cognitive Theory, Research and Therapy. New York: Guilford Press; 2008.

8. NHS Foundation Trust: Institute of Psychiatry. Paranoid thoughts. 2012.

http://www.paranoidthoughts.com. Accessed October 30, 2013.

9. Haddock G, McCarron J, Tarrier N, Faragher EB. Scales to measure dimensions of hallucinations and delusions: the Psychotic Symptom Rating Scales (PSYRATS). Psychol Med. 1999;29:879-889.

10. Myers E, Startup H, Freeman D. Cognitive behavioural treatment of insomnia in individuals with persistent persecutory delusions: a pilot trial. J Behav Ther Exp Psychiatry. 2011;42:330-336.

11. Foster C, Startup H, Potts L, Freeman D. A randomised controlled trial of a worry intervention for individuals with persistent persecutory delusions.J Behav Ther Exp Psychiatry. 2010;41:45-51.

12. Schulze K, Freeman D, Green C, Kuipers E. Intrusive mental imagery in patients with persecutory delusions. Behav Res Ther. 2013;51:7-14.

13. Birchwood M, Gilbert P, Gilbert J, et al. Interpersonal and role-related schema influence the relationship with the dominant "voice" in schizophrenia: a comparison of three models. Psychol Med. 2004;34:1571-1580.

14.Addington D, Jean Addington MD and Patten S. Relapse rates in an early psychosis treatment service. Acta Psychiatrica Scandinavica 2007; 115: 126-131.

15.*Alvarez-Jimenez M, Priede A, Hetrick SE et al. Risk factors for relapse following*

treatment for first episode psychosis: a systematic review

16.*Clinical practice in early psychosis Preventing relapse in first episode psychosis https://www.orygen.org.au/Training/Resources/Psychosis/Clinical-practice-points/Preventing-relapse-in-FEP/Preventing-relapse-in-first-episode-psychosis[online;asssessed 02/02/2020]*

Crisis helplines and support groups

United Kingdom:

Samaritans: Call 116 123 (available 24/7)

Mind Infoline: Call 0300 123 3393 (available during weekdays)

CALM (Campaign Against Living Miserably): Call 0800 58 58 58 (available for men, evenings, and weekends)

SANEline: Call 0300 304 7000 (available evenings)

United States:

National Suicide Prevention Lifeline: Call 1-800-273-TALK (1-800-273-8255) (available 24/7)

Crisis Text Line: Text "HELLO" to 741741 (available 24/7)

NAMI (National Alliance on Mental Illness) Helpline: Call 1-800-950-NAMI (1-800-950-6264) (available during weekdays)

Canada:

Crisis Services Canada: Call 1-833-456-4566 (available 24/7)

Kids Help Phone: Call 1-800-668-6868 (available for youth, 24/7)

Canadian Association for Suicide Prevention: Visit
https://suicideprevention.ca/ to find local crisis centers

Australia:
Lifeline Australia: Call 13 11 14 (available 24/7)

Beyond Blue: Call 1300 22 4636 (available 24/7)

Kids Helpline: Call 1800 55 1800 (available for children
and teenagers, 24/7)

South Africa:
Suicide Crisis Helpline: Call 0800 567 567 (available
24/7)

SADAG Mental Health Line: Call 011 234 4837
(available 24/7)

Childline South Africa: Call 08000 55 555 (available for
children, 24/7)

Europe (varying by country):

France:
SOS Suicide: Call 01 45 39 40 00 (available 24/7)

Germany:
Telefonseelsorge: Call 0800 111 0 111 or 0800 111 0
222 (available 24/7)

Netherlands:
113 Zelfmoordpreventie: Call 0800 0113 (available
24/7)

Spain:

Teléfono de la Esperanza: Call 717 003 717 (available 24/7)

Remember, if you or someone you know is in immediate danger or experiencing a mental health crisis, it's crucial to seek help from a professional or call emergency services in your country.

Glossary of common mental health terms:

Anxiety: A feeling of unease, worry, or fear, which can be mild or severe. It is a normal response to stress but can become a disorder when it significantly interferes with daily life.

Bipolar disorder: A mental health condition characterized by extreme mood swings, including episodes of mania (elevated mood, increased energy, and reduced need for sleep) and depression.

Cognitive-behavioral therapy (CBT): A type of psychotherapy that focuses on identifying and changing negative thought patterns and behaviors to improve emotional well-being.

Depression: A mental health disorder characterized by persistent feelings of sadness, hopelessness, and a lack of interest or pleasure in activities.

Eating disorder: A group of mental health conditions characterized by abnormal eating habits, such as anorexia nervosa, bulimia nervosa, and binge eating disorder.

Major depressive disorder (MDD): A more severe form of depression, characterized by a persistent low mood and loss of interest in activities, leading to significant impairment in daily life.

Mania: A phase of bipolar disorder marked by an abnormally elevated mood, increased energy, and reduced need for sleep.

Mindfulness: A mental state achieved by focusing one's awareness on the present moment, while calmly acknowledging and accepting one's feelings, thoughts, and bodily sensations.

Obsessive-compulsive disorder (OCD): A mental health disorder characterized by recurrent, unwanted thoughts (obsessions) and/or repetitive behaviors (compulsions) that are difficult to control.

Panic disorder: A type of anxiety disorder characterized by recurrent, unexpected panic attacks, which are episodes of intense fear accompanied by physical symptoms.

Post-traumatic stress disorder (PTSD): A mental health condition that can develop after experiencing or witnessing a traumatic event, characterized by flashbacks, nightmares, and severe anxiety.

Psychologist: A mental health professional who specializes in the assessment, diagnosis, and treatment of mental health disorders using various therapeutic techniques.

Psychiatrist: A medical doctor who specializes in the diagnosis, treatment, and prevention of mental health disorders, including the prescription of medications.

Psychotherapy: A general term for the treatment of mental health disorders through various therapeutic techniques, which can include talk therapy, cognitive-behavioural therapy, and other approaches.

Schizophrenia: A severe mental health disorder characterized by disordered thoughts, perceptions, and emotions, which can result in hallucinations, delusions, and disorganized behaviour.

Self-care: The practice of taking care of one's physical, emotional, and mental well-being through various activities and strategies.

Social anxiety disorder: A type of anxiety disorder characterized by an intense fear of social situations and a fear of being negatively judged or scrutinized by others.

Stress: A physical, mental, or emotional factor that causes bodily or mental tension and can be a factor in the development of mental health disorders.

Substance use disorder: A mental health condition characterized by the harmful use of substances, such as drugs or alcohol, resulting in negative consequences and impairment in daily life.

Trauma: An emotional response to a deeply distressing or disturbing event that can have lasting effects on mental health and well-being.

Resilience: The ability to adapt and recover from adversity, stress, or trauma, and maintain or regain mental well-being.

Dialectical behaviour therapy (DBT): A type of cognitive-behavioural therapy that helps individuals develop skills to cope with and manage intense emotions, improve relationships, and reduce self-destructive behaviours.

Emotional intelligence: The ability to identify, understand, and manage one's own emotions and those of others.

Generalized anxiety disorder (GAD): A type of anxiety disorder characterized by persistent and excessive worry about various aspects of life, often interfering with daily functioning.

Mental health: The state of emotional, psychological, and social well-being, affecting how individuals think, feel, and act.

Mindfulness-based stress reduction (MBSR): A structured program that combines mindfulness meditation and yoga to help individuals manage stress, anxiety, and chronic pain.

Mood disorders: A category of mental health disorders characterized by disturbances in mood, including major depressive disorder and bipolar disorder.

Personality disorders: A group of mental health conditions characterized by enduring patterns of maladaptive thoughts, feelings, and behaviours that can cause significant distress and impair daily functioning.

Positive psychology: The scientific study of what makes life worth living, focusing on human strengths, virtues, and optimal functioning.

Psychosocial: Referring to the interrelation of social factors and individual thoughts, emotions, and behaviours.

Self-compassion: The practice of treating oneself with kindness and understanding, particularly during times of stress or failure.

Stigma: Negative attitudes and beliefs about individuals with mental health disorders, leading to discrimination and social exclusion.

Support groups: Groups of individuals who share a common experience, such as a mental health condition, and provide mutual support, encouragement, and understanding.

Trauma-informed care: An approach to mental health treatment that recognizes the impact of trauma on an individual's mental health and integrates this understanding into treatment planning and delivery.

Wellness: The state of being in good health, both physically and mentally, achieved through a balance of various factors, such as exercise, nutrition, and self-care practices.

Adjustment disorder: A stress-related mental health condition that occurs when an individual has difficulty coping with or adjusting to a significant life change or stressor.

Attention deficit hyperactivity disorder (ADHD): A neurodevelopmental disorder characterized by inattention, impulsivity, and hyperactivity, affecting both children and adults.

Borderline personality disorder (BPD): A mental health disorder characterized by unstable moods, self-image, and relationships, as well as impulsive behaviours and difficulties with emotional regulation.

Cognitive distortions: Irrational or unhelpful thought patterns that can contribute to negative emotions and mental health issues.

Coping strategies: Techniques and behaviours used to manage stress, emotional pain, and challenging situations.

Made in the USA
Monee, IL
06 August 2024

63317379R00046